JOHN MAYER HEAVIER THINGS

Transcribed by Jeff Jacobson,
under the supervision of John Mayer

Album art direction by John Mayer
Graphics by Ames Design
Album artwork courtesy of Sony Records
Cover photo by Chapman Baehler

Cherry Lane Music Company
Director of Publications/Project Editor: Mark Phillips
Manager of Publications: Rebecca Quigley

ISBN 1-57560-733-6

Visit our website at www.cherrylane.com

JOHN MAYER GETS INTO SOME *HEAVIER THINGS*

When John Mayer emerged from the underground in 2001 with his debut album, *Room for Squares*, he was a little-known 22-year-old with an acoustic guitar and boundless energy. His ascent was rapid, powered by nonstop touring and intensive word of mouth, which reached critical mass just as radio and the video channels were discovering the young artist. Two years later, *Room for Squares* was triple-platinum (the album remained in the Top 100 after more than 80 consecutive weeks on the *Billboard* Top 200 chart), spawning three hit singles, one of which, "Your Body Is a Wonderland," earned him a Grammy in 2003 for Best Pop Vocal Performance.

Mayer's much-anticipated Aware/Columbia follow-up album, which bears the intriguing title *Heavier Things*, demonstrates how far this single-minded artist has come at this still-early stage of his career.

"In some ways," Mayer says, "the stakes get higher when you make a second major-label record and everyone's looking. And in some ways absolutely nothing is different, because your voice still sounds the same, and your hands still feel the same on the guitar. You just write your songs. You're just a guy with a guitar putting in a Thai food order at 9 p.m."

The 25-year-old Mayer possesses a remarkable clear-headedness—fittingly, the new album opens with a song titled "Clarity"—and the rarefied level of consciousness that distinguishes this artist's songs has as much to do with their impact as his gift for melody, elevated musicianship, or disarming personality. All of these elements, by the way, are present in spades on *Heavier Things*.

The album was produced and mixed by Jack Joseph Puig, whose credits include Sheryl Crow, No Doubt, the Black Crowes, Hole, and smart-pop progenitors Jellyfish.

"Jack understood what I wanted to do next," Mayer says of his decision to work with Puig. "We had met by way of friendship, not connections. I don't like pulling connections in; I'd much rather make friends. He understands the romance of making records. Jack and I pushed each other to the limits of our knowledge, and that's why the record is as fresh as it is. There are raw decisions made outside of the comfort zone of past achievement."

Heavier Things was tracked in New York, Mayer's present home, and completed at Puig's longtime L.A. headquarters, Ocean Way. In addition to the lead single, the propulsive, hook-packed rocker "Bigger Than My Body," the album contains several songs Mayer performed live on his 2003 summer tour of amphitheaters and arenas—songs that became immediate crowd favorites. These include the poignant "Daughters," the smoldering, blues-based "Come Back to Bed," the evocative "Wheel," and "Something's Missing," which climaxes with a timely and ingenious things-to-do-today inventory.

Mayer's longtime bass player, David LaBruyere, appears on all tracks apart from the virtually solo acoustic "Daughters," while keyboardist Jamie Muhoberac plays on eight. Guest musicians include legendary jazz trumpeter Roy Hargrove, drummers Matt Chamberlain, Steve Jordan, and ?uestlove from the Roots, percussionist Lenny Castro, and horn player Jerry Hay. Also present are guitarist Michael Chaves and drummer J.J. Johnson from Mayer's touring band.

"I came off the road after two years of straight touring and knew exactly what kind of record I wanted to make—it wasn't an accident," Mayer says of the process that led to the creation of *Heavier Things*. "I wanted to write songs this time that always felt good under my hands, no matter what. The only real criterion for the record was, 'Is it fun to play? Is it physically fun to feel the vibration of the strings or the feel of my throat when I'm singing it?' If an idea didn't meet that criterion, it got dumped.

"This record is as different from the last one as I am from the last time I made a record," he adds. "What that amount is, I don't know, and I'm really interested to find out."

KEYWORDS BY SONG

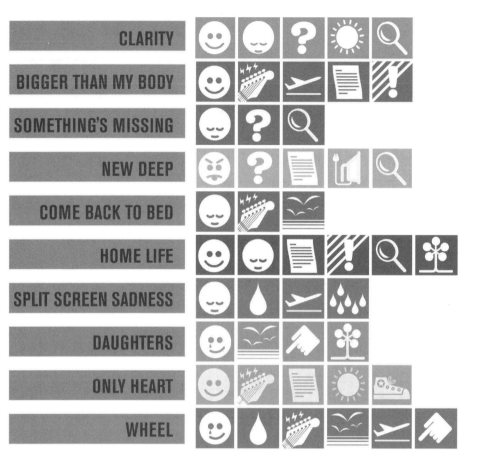

CLARITY

BIGGER THAN MY BODY

SOMETHING'S MISSING

NEW DEEP

COME BACK TO BED

HOME LIFE

SPLIT SCREEN SADNESS

DAUGHTERS

ONLY HEART

WHEEL

CONTENTS

Key

SARCASTIC	OPTIMISTIC	BITTERSWEET	PENSIVE	LOVE LOST	GUITAR SOLO
BALLAD	FLIGHT	QUIZZICAL	PROMISSORY	IRONIC	SUNNY
RAINY	DEFIANT	ADVICE	SEARCHING	RETRO	FAMILY

CLARITY

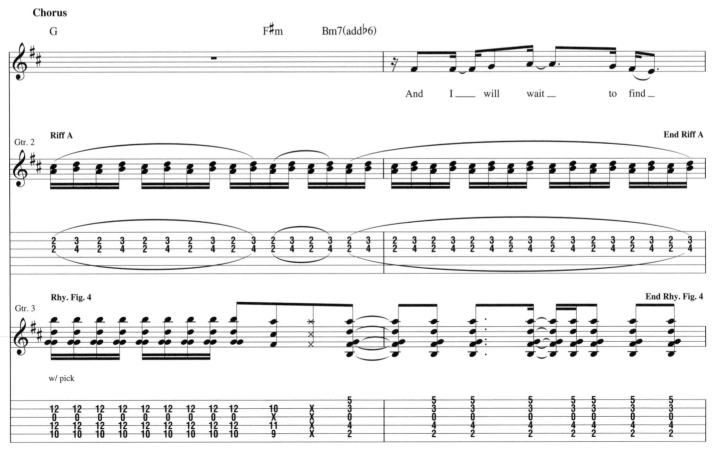

6

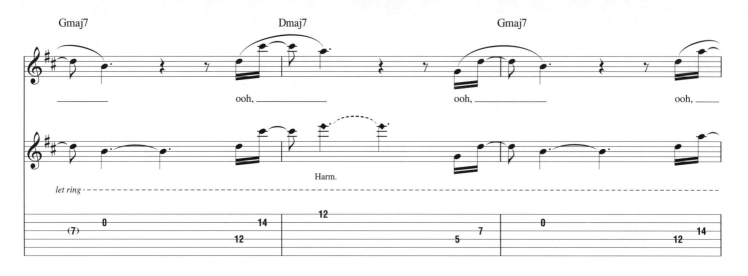

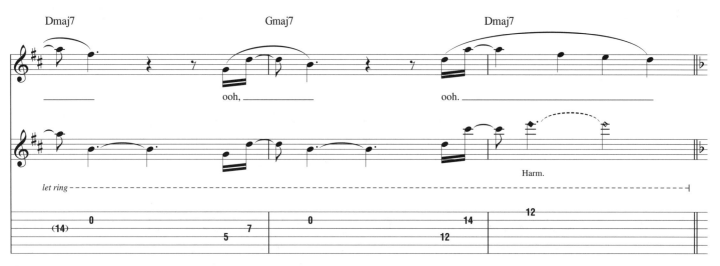

Interlude

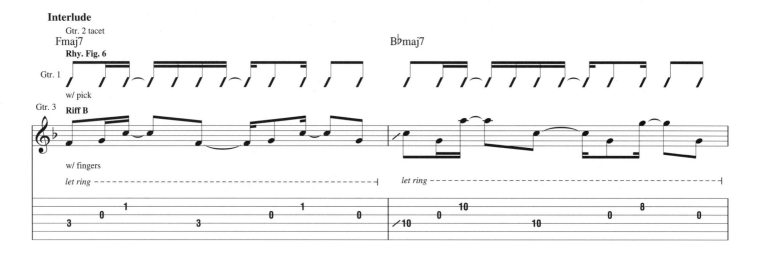

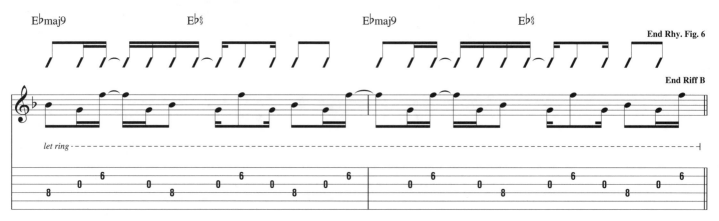

Bridge

Gtr. 1: w/ Rhy. Fig. 6 (2 times)
Gtr. 3: w/ Riff B (2 times)

So much wast - ed in _____ the af - ter - noon.

So much sa - cred in _____ the month _____

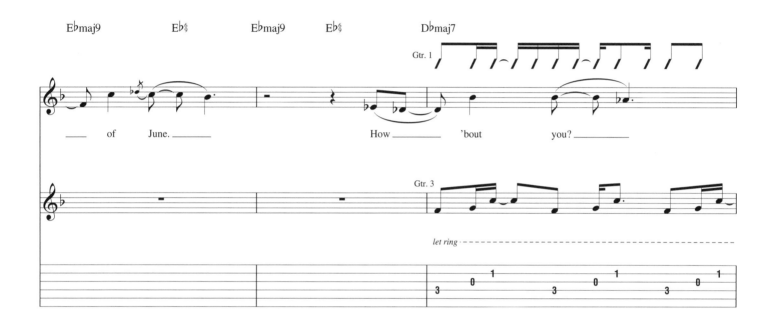

_____ of June. _____ How _____ 'bout you? _____

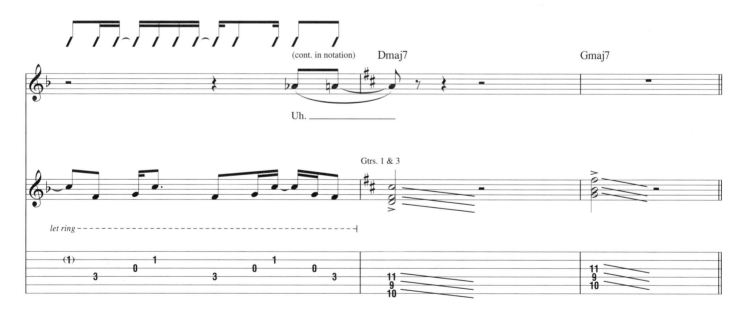

Uh. _____

Outro-Chorus

Gtr. 2: w/ Riff A (till end)
Gtr. 3: w/ Rhy. Fig. 4 (till end)

And I _____ will wait _____ to find _____

if this will last for - ev - er. And I will wait to find

that it won't and it won't, and it won't.

And I won't pay no mind wor - ried 'bout no rain - y weath - er.

And I will waste no time re - main -

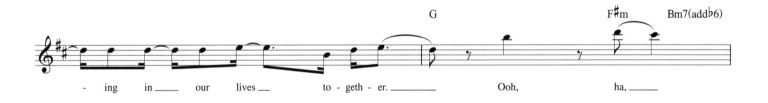

- ing in our lives to - geth - er. Ooh, ha,

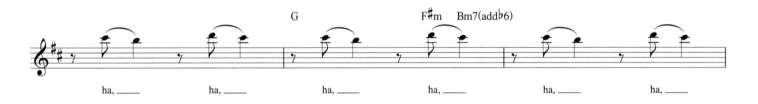

ha, ha, ha, ha, ha, ha,

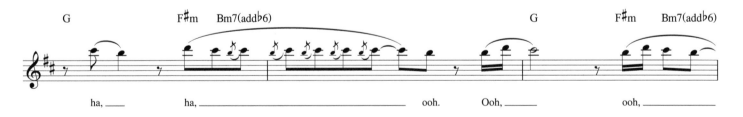

ha, ha, ooh. Ooh, ooh,

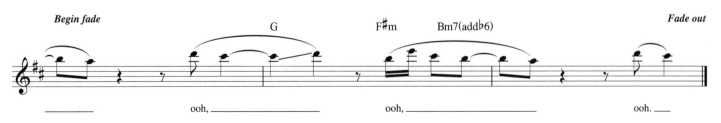

ooh, ooh, ooh.

BIGGER THAN MY BODY

Words and Music by
John Mayer

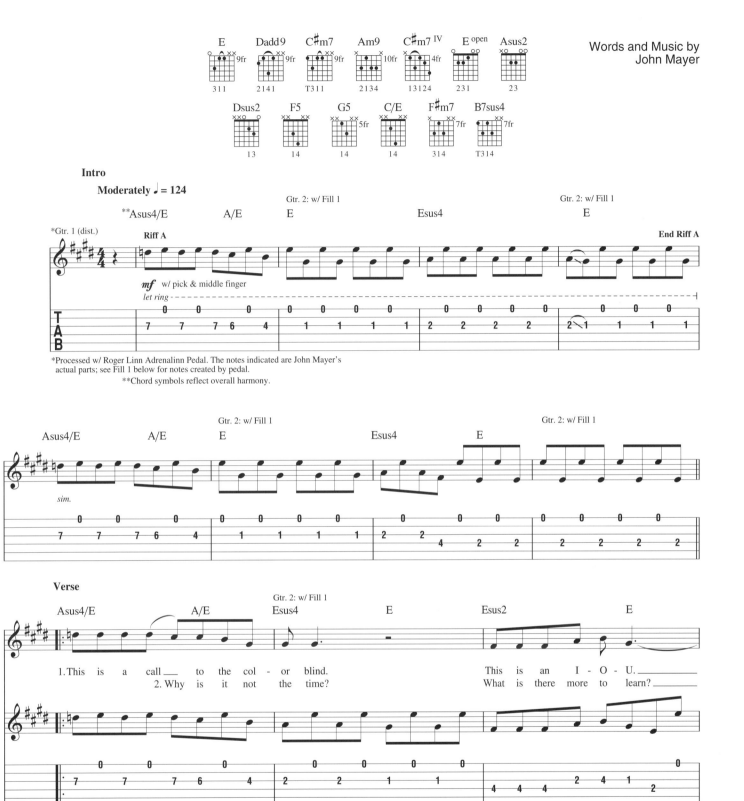

*Processed w/ Roger Linn Adrenalinn Pedal. The notes indicated are John Mayer's
actual parts; see Fill 1 below for notes created by pedal.

**Chord symbols reflect overall harmony.

1. This is a call ___ to the col - or blind.
2. Why is it not the time?

This is an I - O - U. ___
What is there more to learn? ___

**The notes indicated in Fill 1 are not actually played,
but are created by Adrenalinn Pedal.
***Adrenalinn Pedal arr. for gtr.

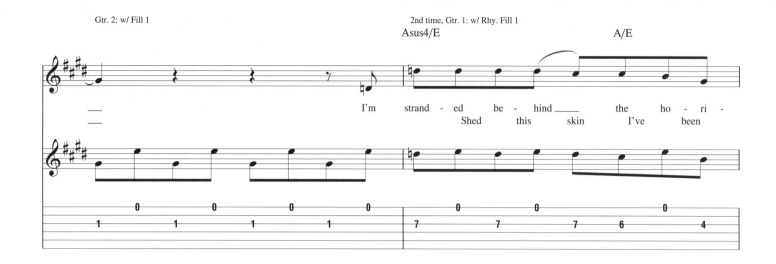

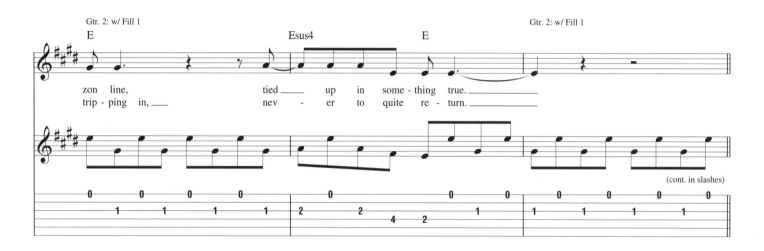

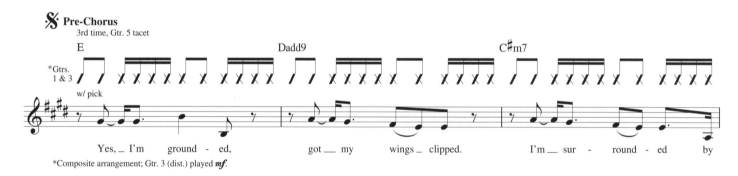

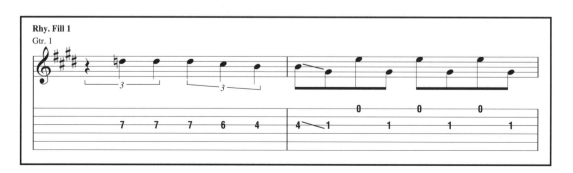

SOMETHING'S MISSING

Words and Music by
John Mayer

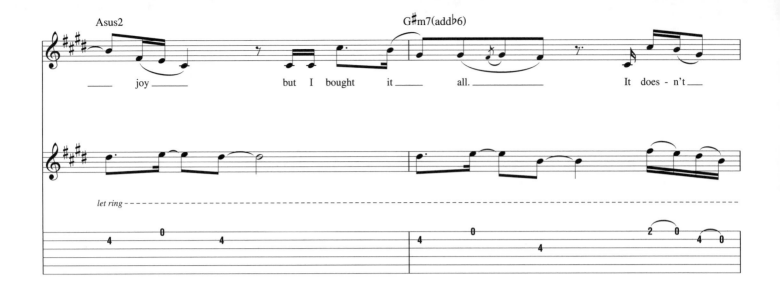

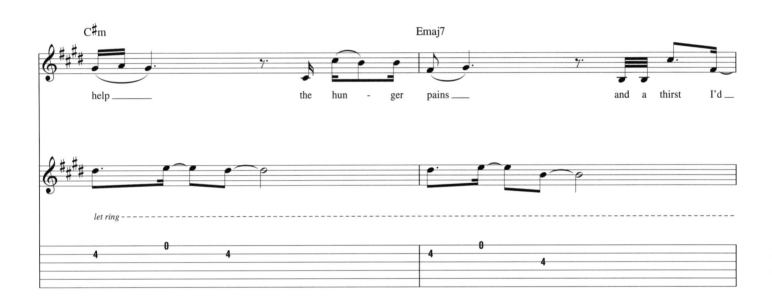

18

Asus2   Bsus$\frac{2}{4}$ Bsus4

don't know ___ what it is.   No, I   don't   know ___ what it is _____ at all. ___

Gtrs. 1 & 2: w/ Rhy. Figs. 1 & 1A

N.C.   C#m11   N.C.   C#m11   N.C.

___   3. When   au - tumn ___

Verse

Gtr. 1: w/ Rhy. Fig. 2 (2 times)

C#m   Emaj7   Asus2

___ comes,   it does - n't   ask; __   it just walks _ in ____   where it left   you ___

Gtr. 2

let ring -

G#m7(add♭6)   C#m   Emaj7

___ last. ___   You nev - er   know ___   when it   starts _   un - til there's

let ring -

D.S. al Coda

Asus2   G#m7(add♭6)

fog   in - side   the   glass _ a - round _____   your sum - mer   heart. ___

let ring -

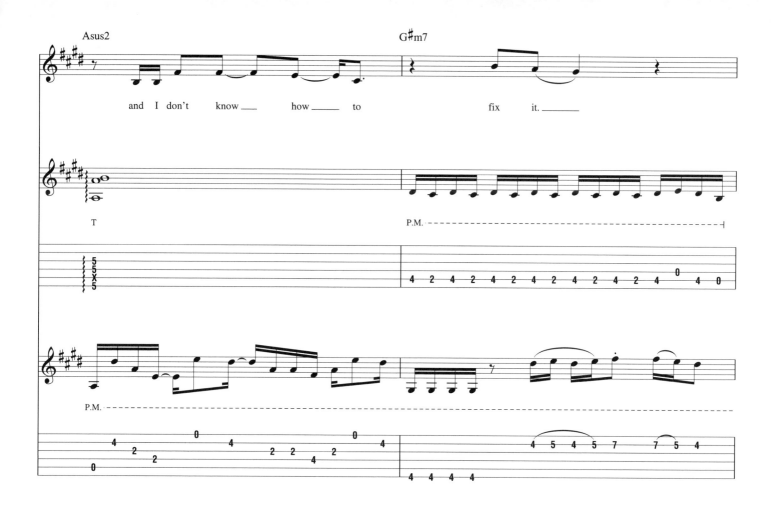

and I don't know ___ how ___ to   fix   it. ___

Some - thing's ___   miss - ing ___   and I

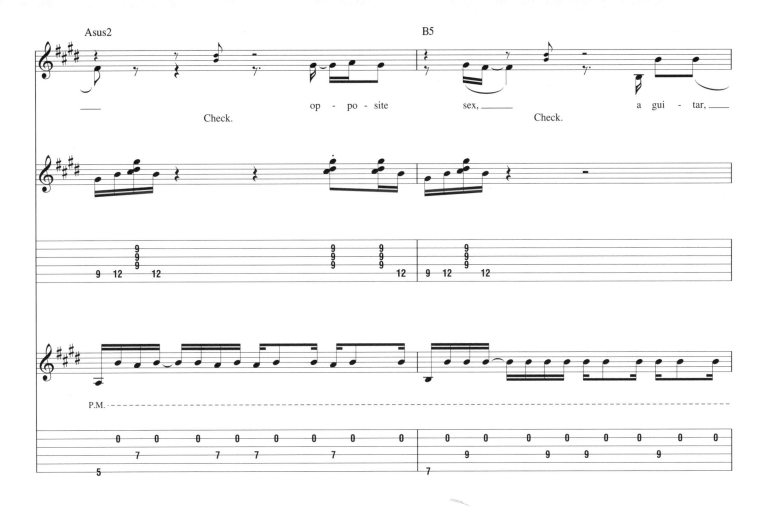

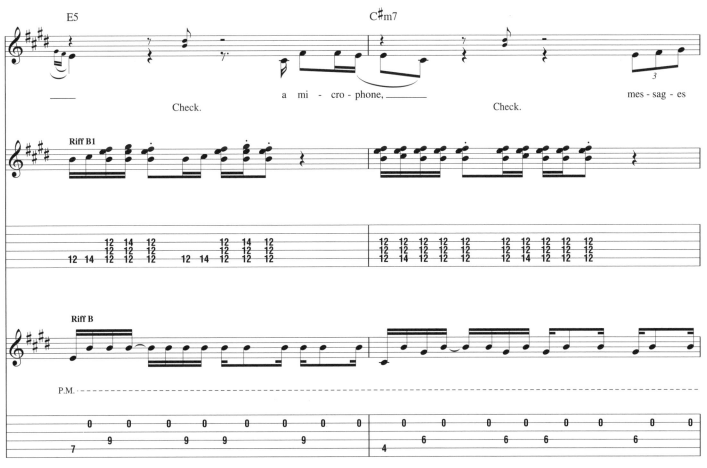

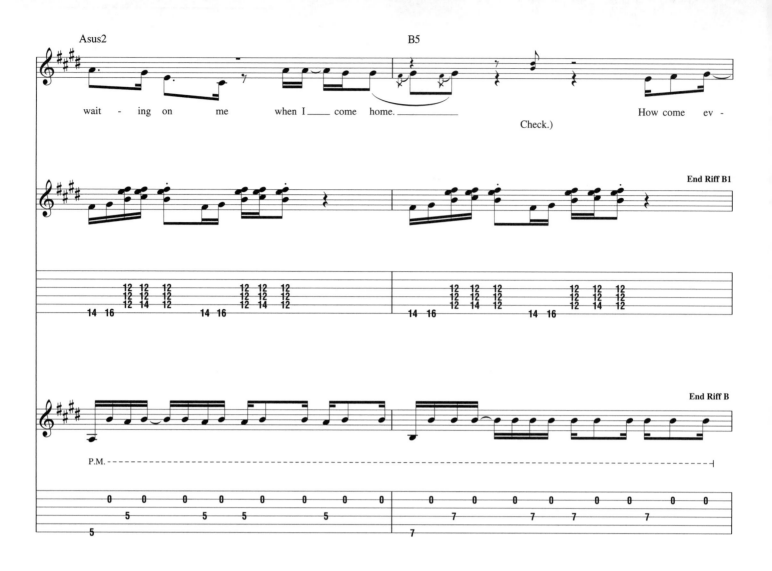

waiting on me when I ___ come home. ___ (Check.) How come ev -

End Riff B1

End Riff B

Begin fade

Gtrs. 2 & 3: w/ Riffs B & B1 (1 1/2 times)

E5   C#m7

- 'ry - thing ___ I think I need   al - ways comes ___ with bat - ter - ies? Ah. _____

Asus2   B5

___   What do you think ___ it means? ___   How come ev -

Fade out

E5   C#m7

- 'ry - thing ___ I think I need   al - ways comes ___ with bat - ter - ies?

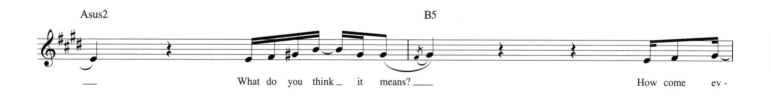

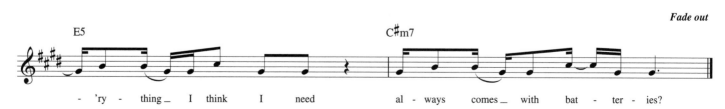

26

NEW DEEP

Words and Music by
John Mayer

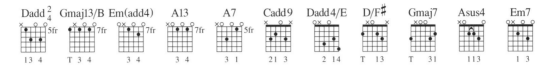

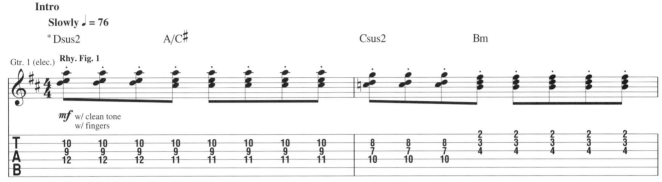

Intro

Slowly ♩ = 76

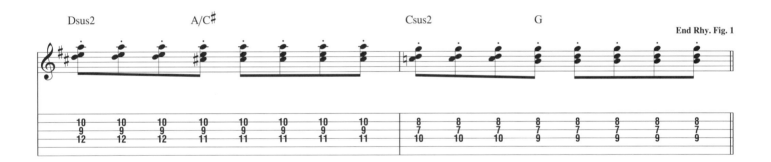

*Chord symbols reflect overall harmony.

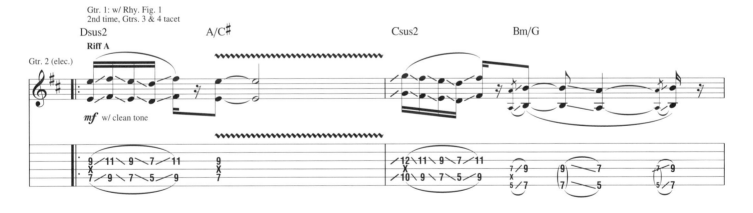

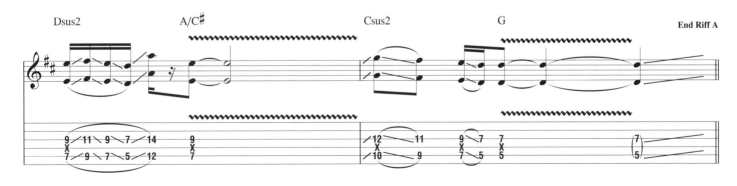

Verse

Gtr. 1: w/ Rhy. Fig. 1 (2 3/4 times)
Gtr. 2 tacet
2nd time, Gtr. 5: w/ Rhy. Fig. 2 (4 times)

1. I'm so a - live.   I'm so en - light - ened. I can
2. Is there a God?   Why is he wait - ing? Don't you

bare - ly sur - vive   a night in my mind. So
think of it odd   when he knows my ad - dress? And

I've got a plan.   I'm gon - na find out just how
look at the stars.   Don't it re - mind you just how

bor - ing I am   and have a good time. 'Cause ev - er since I
fee - ble we are?   Well, it used to, I guess.

tried try - ing not to find ev - 'ry lit - tle mean - ing in my life, it's been fine.

I've been cool with my new gold - en rule. Numb is the

Gtr. 1

Rhy. Fig. 2

Gtr. 5 (acous.)

mf w/ fingers

let ring - - - -   let ring - - - - - - - - -   let ring - - - -   let ring - - - - - - - - - -

28

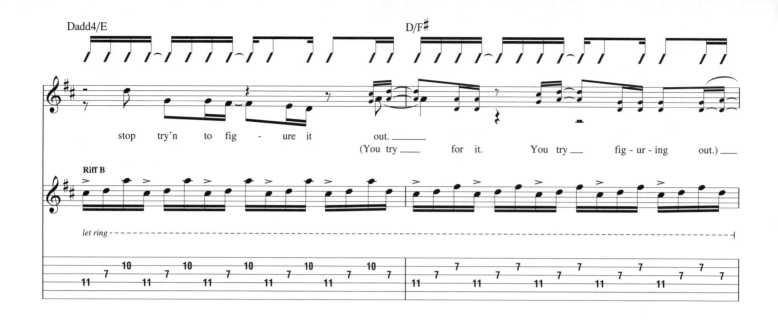

stop try'n to fig - ure it out. _____ (You try _____ for it. You try _____ fig - ur - ing out.) _____

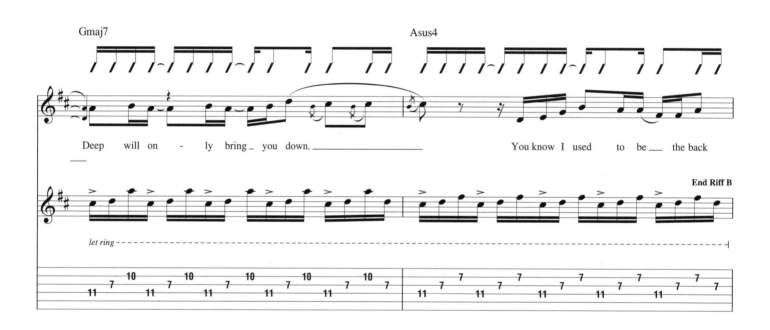

Deep will on - ly bring _ you down. _____ You know I used to be _ the back

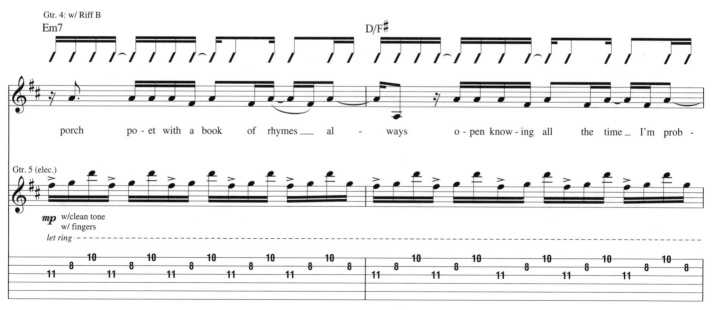

porch po - et with a book of rhymes _ al - ways o - pen know-ing all the time _ I'm prob -

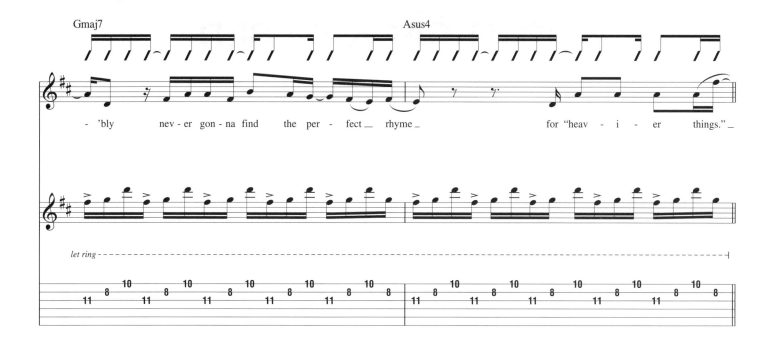

-'bly nev - er gon - na find the per - fect _ rhyme _ for "heav - i - er things." _

let ring

Outro

Gtr. 1: w/ Rhy. Fig. 1
Gtr. 2: w/ Riff A
Gtr. 5 tacet

Gtr. 1: w/ Rhy. Fig. 1

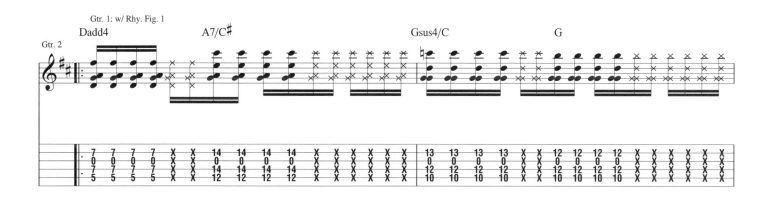

Repeat and fade

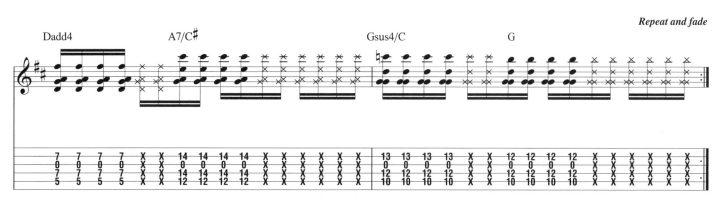

COME BACK TO BED

Words and Music by
John Mayer

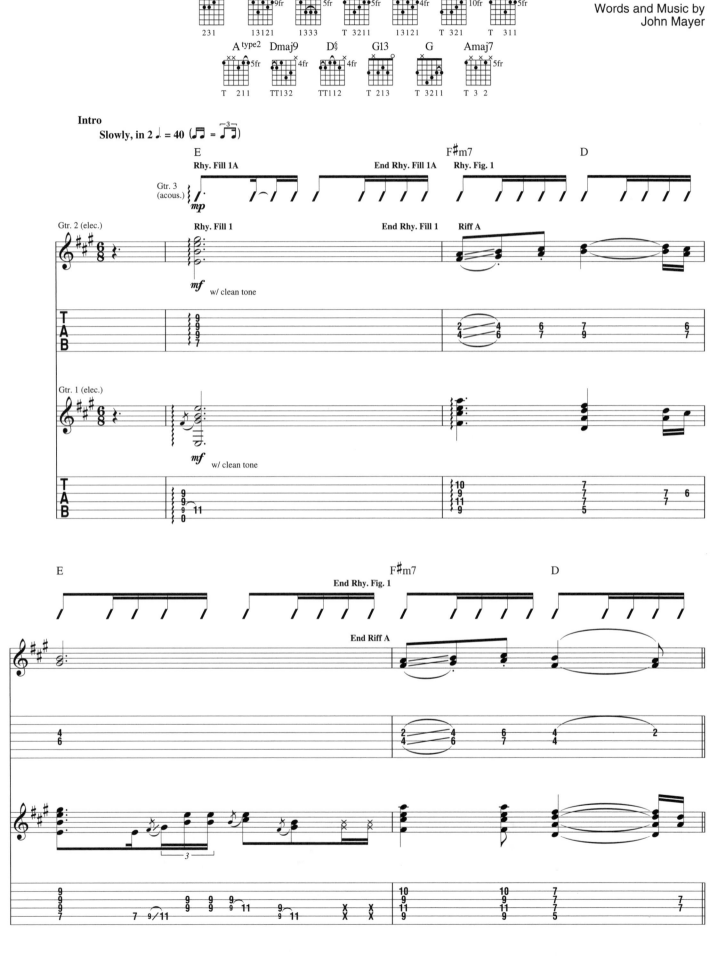

sheets

and your foot - steps   are   down the   hall.

So   tell   me   what   I _____ did.   I   can't   find   where   the   mo - ment   went

wrong   at   all.   You ___ can   be   mad   in   the   morn - ing.

I'll   take   back   what   I   said.   Just   don't   leave ___

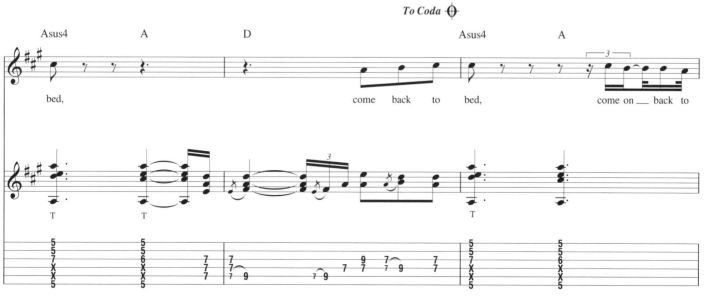

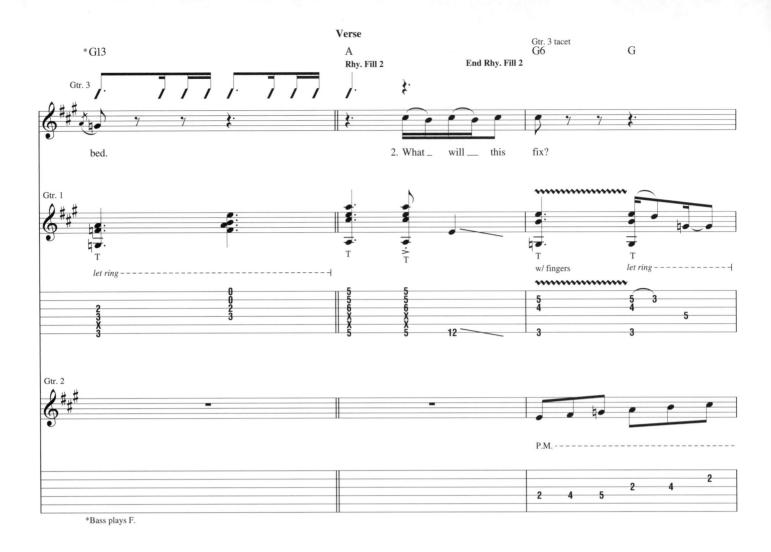

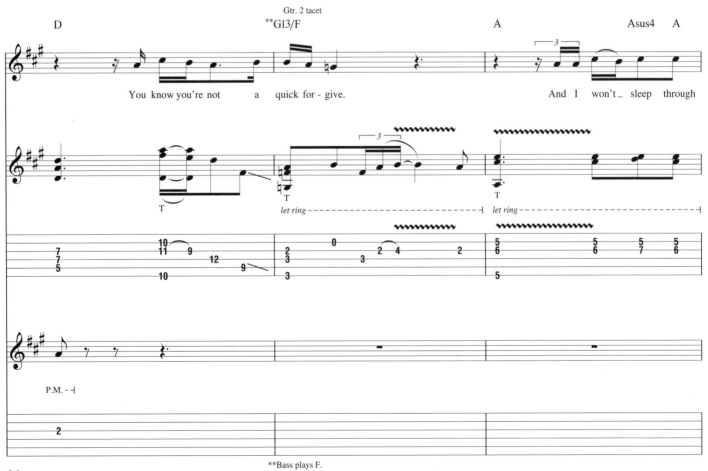

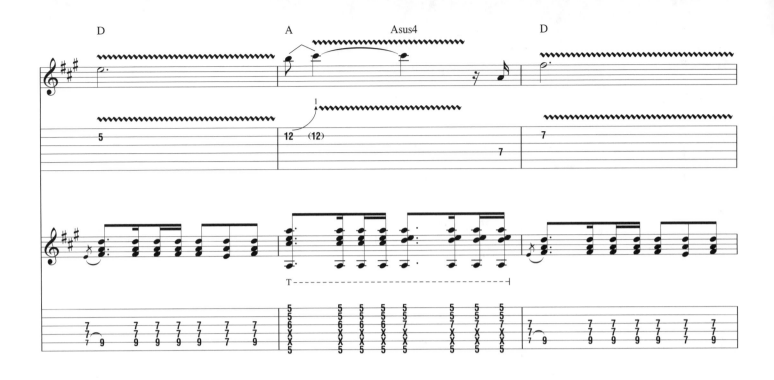

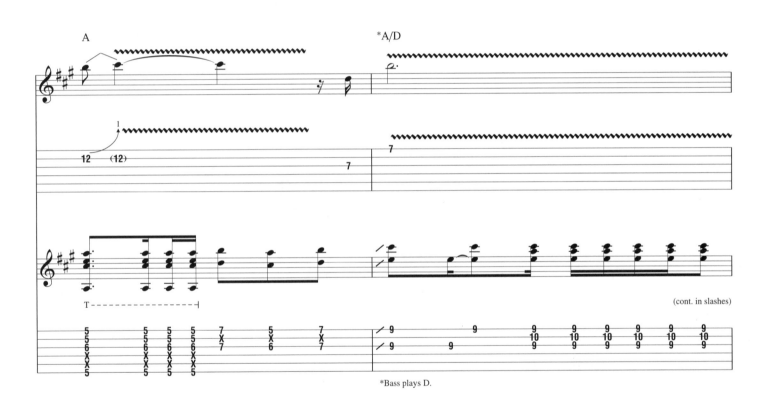

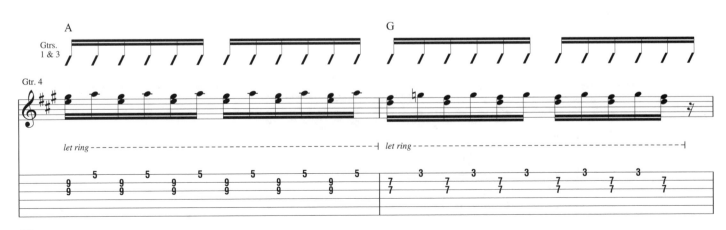

HOME LIFE

Words by John Mayer
Music by John Mayer
and David LaBreyure

(Csus2) (F⁶/₉) (C) (A) (Bm7add4) (Fsus2) (Em7add4)

Gtrs. 1, 4 & 7: Tune down 1 step:
(low to high) D-G-C-F-A-D

Intro

Moderately slow ♩ = 108

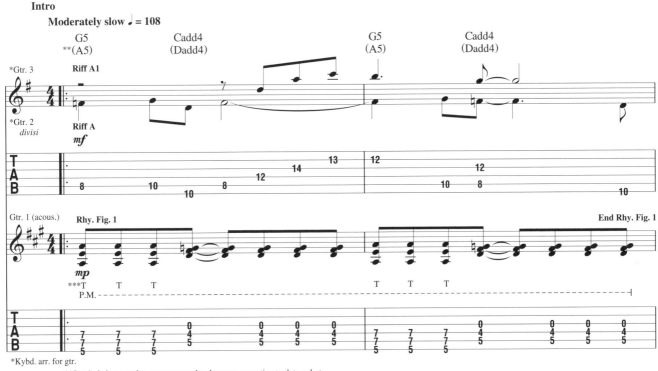

*Kybd. arr. for gtr.

**Symbols in parentheses represent chord names respective to detuned gtr.
Symbols above reflect actual sounding chords.

***T = Thumb on 6th string

Gtr. 1: w/ Rhy. Fig. 1

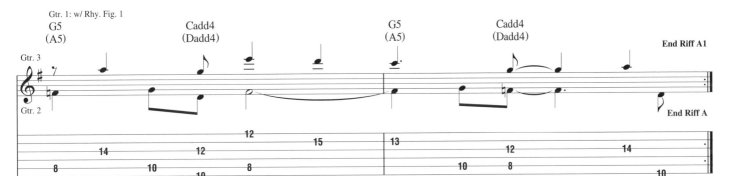

Verse

Gtr. 1: w/ Rhy. Fig. 1 (8 times)
Gtrs. 2 & 3: w/ Riffs A & A1 (4 1/2 times)

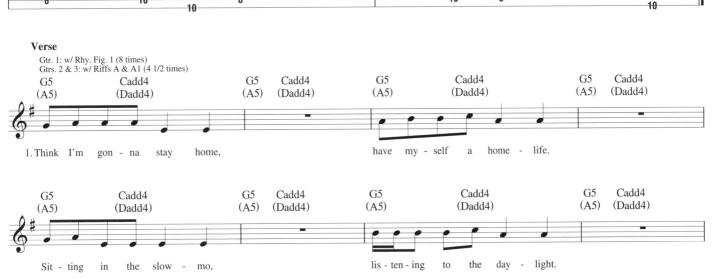

1. Think I'm gon-na stay home, have my-self a home-life.

Sit-ting in the slow-mo, lis-ten-ing to the day-light.

Nev - er to lead ___ me to an - y - thing re - mote - ly close to a home ___

Chorus

Gtr. 1: w/ Rhy. Fig. 3
Gtr. 6: w/ Riff C

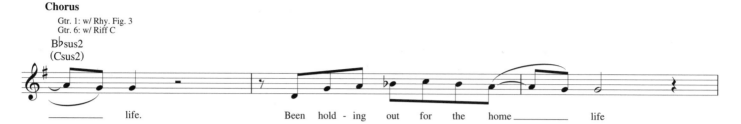

___ life. Been hold - ing out for the home ___ life

Gtrs. 1 & 4: w/ Rhy. Figs. 1 & 2 (2 times)

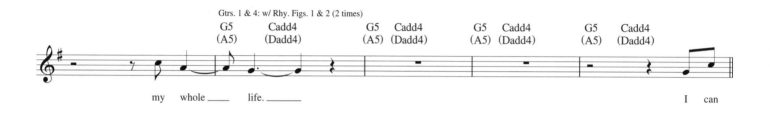

my whole ___ life. ___ I can

Bridge

tell you this much. I will mar - ry just once. And if it does - n't work out, give her
go to my grave with the life that I gave, not just some mel - o - dy line on a

1.

half of my stuff. It's fine with me. We said e - ter -
ra - di - o wave. It dis -

48

SPLIT SCREEN SADNESS

Words and Music by
John Mayer

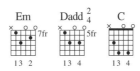

Intro

Moderately ♩ = 112

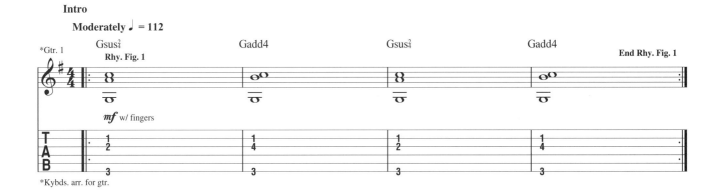

*Kybds. arr. for gtr.

Verse

Gtr. 1: w/ Rhy. Fig. 1

1. And I don't know ___ where you went when you left me, but says here ___ in the wa-

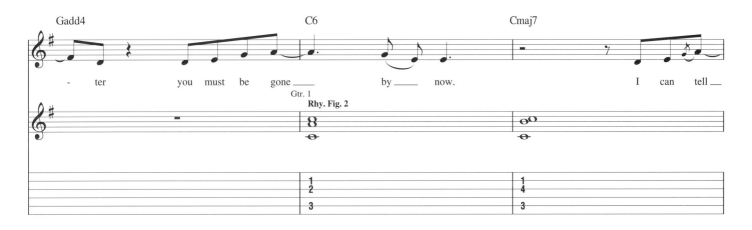

-ter you must be gone ___ by ___ now. I can tell ___

Gtr. 1: w/ Rhy. Fig. 1

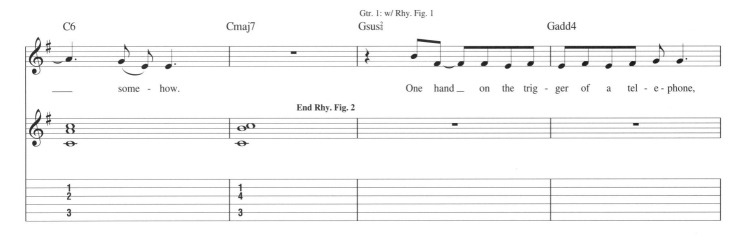

___ some - how. One hand ___ on the trig - ger of a tel - e - phone,

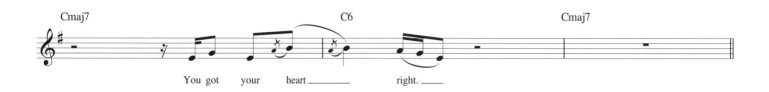

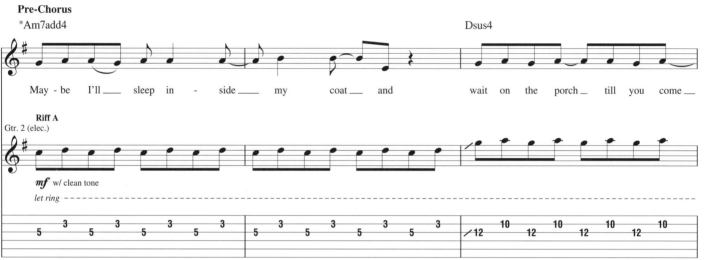

*Chord symbols reflect overall harmony.

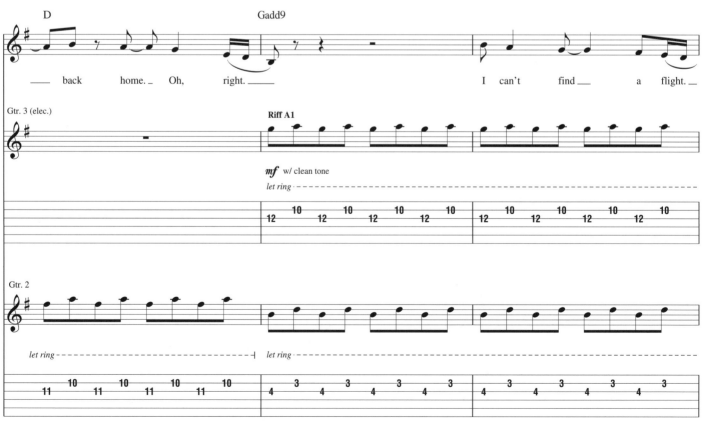

52

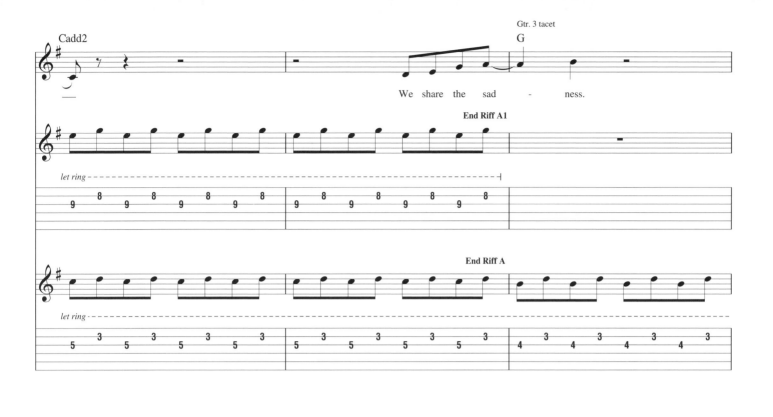

We share the sad - ness.

Split - screen sad - ness.

Chorus

Two wrongs make it all al - right ___ to - night.

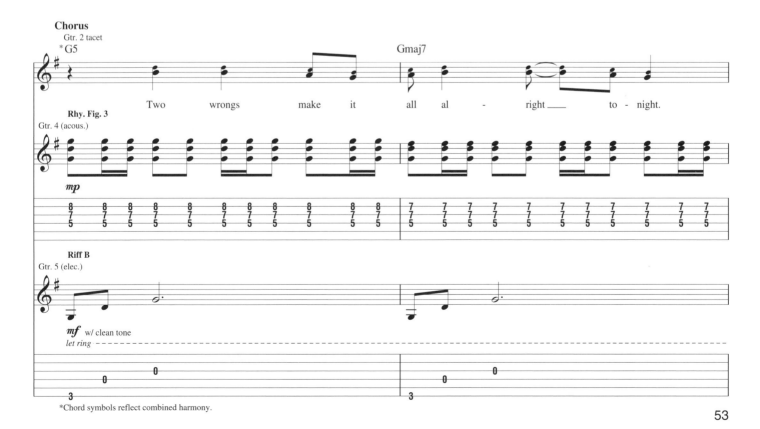

*Chord symbols reflect combined harmony.

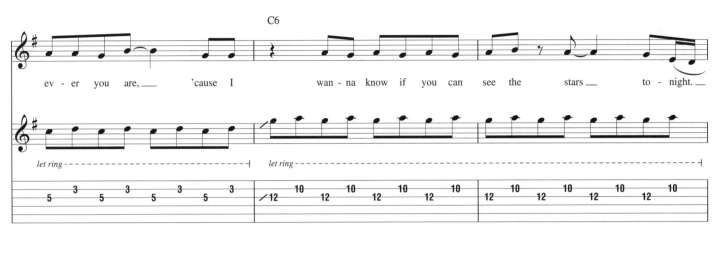

C6

ev - er you are, ___ 'cause I ___ wan - na know if you can see the stars ___ to - night. ___

let ring - - - - - - - - - - - - - - -| *let ring* - |

Gtr. 3: w/ Riff A1

G   Csus2

It might be my ___ on - ly ___ right. ___

let ring -| *let ring* -

𝄋 Chorus

Gtr. 4: w/ Rhy. Fig. 3
Gtr. 5: w/ Riff B
2nd time, Gtr. 2 tacet (next 7 meas.)

G

We share the sad - - - ness.   Split - screen sad -
(Two wrongs make it all al - right ___ to - night.

End Riff D

let ring -| *let ring* -

Cmaj9

- ness.   We share the sad - - - ness.   Two wrongs make it
Two wrongs make it all al - right ___ to - night.

let ring -| *let ring* -

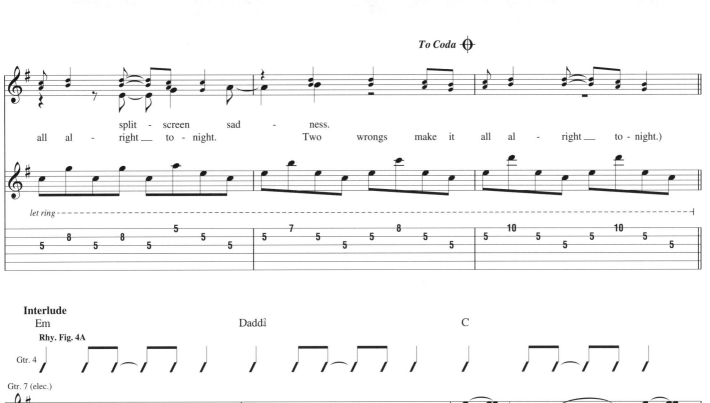

To Coda ✛

all al - right___ to - night.   Two wrongs make it all al - right___ to - night.)

let ring -

Interlude

Em   Dadd$\frac{9}{4}$ C

Rhy. Fig. 4A

Gtr. 4

Gtr. 7 (elec.)

mf w/ clean tone

Rhy. Fig. 4

Gtr. 2

let ring -

Gtrs. 2 & 4: w/ Rhy. Figs. 4 & 4A

Em   Dadd$\frac{9}{4}$

End Rhy. Fig. 4A

P.M. - - - - - - - ┘

End Rhy. Fig. 4

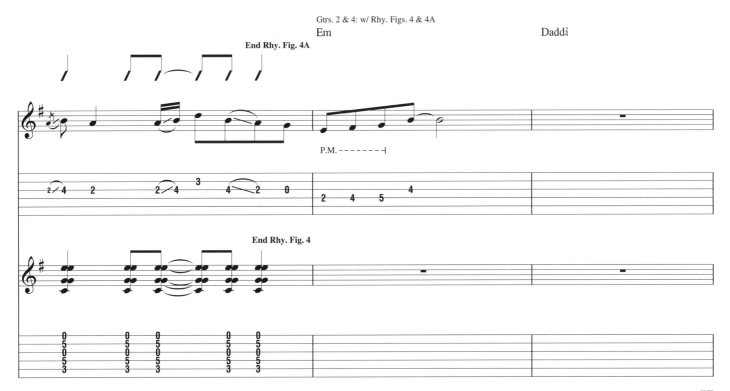

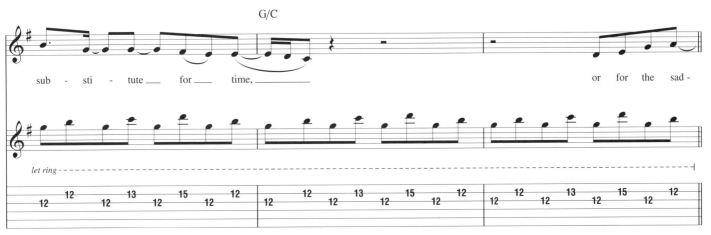

DAUGHTERS

Words and Music by
John Mayer

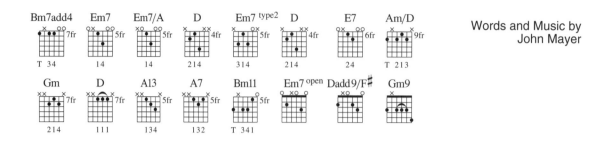

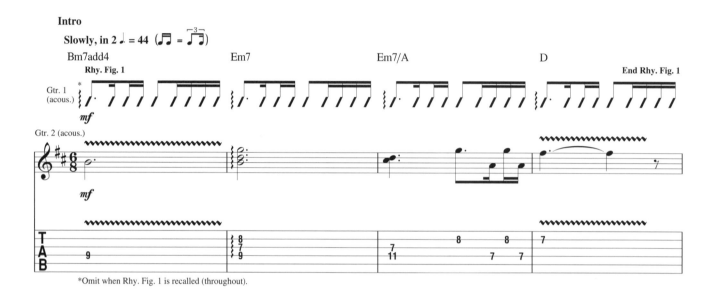

Intro

Slowly, in 2 ♩ = 44

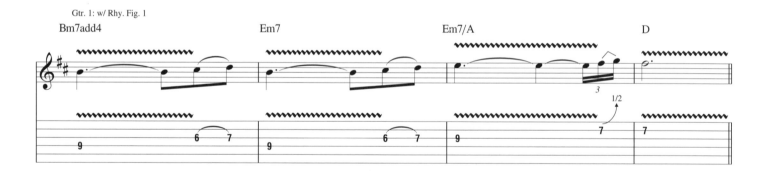

*Omit when Rhy. Fig. 1 is recalled (throughout).

Gtr. 1: w/ Rhy. Fig. 1

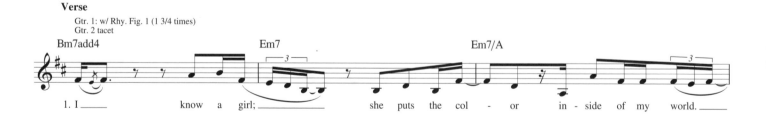

Verse

Gtr. 1: w/ Rhy. Fig. 1 (1 3/4 times)
Gtr. 2 tacet

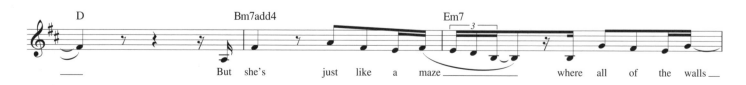

1. I ___ know a girl; ___ she puts the col- or in- side of my world. ___

But she's just like a maze ___ where all of the walls ___

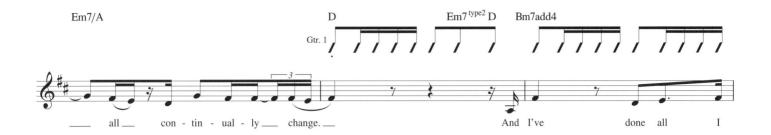

all con-tin-ual-ly change. And I've done all I

can to stand on her steps with my heart in my hand. Now

I'm start-ing to see may-be it's got noth-ing to do with me.

⅍ Chorus

2nd & 3rd times, Bkgd. Voc.: w/ Voc. Fig. 1 (4 times)

Fa - thers, be good to your daugh - ters.

1st time, Gtr. 1: w/ Rhy. Fig. 2 (2 1/2 times)
2nd & 3rd times, Gtr. 1: w/ Rhy. Fig. 2 (3 times)

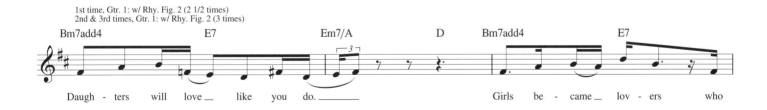

Daugh-ters will love like you do. Girls be-came lov-ers who

Voc. Fig. 1

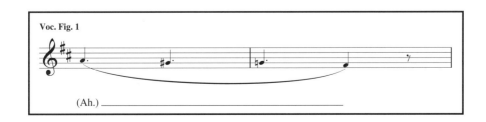

(Ah.)

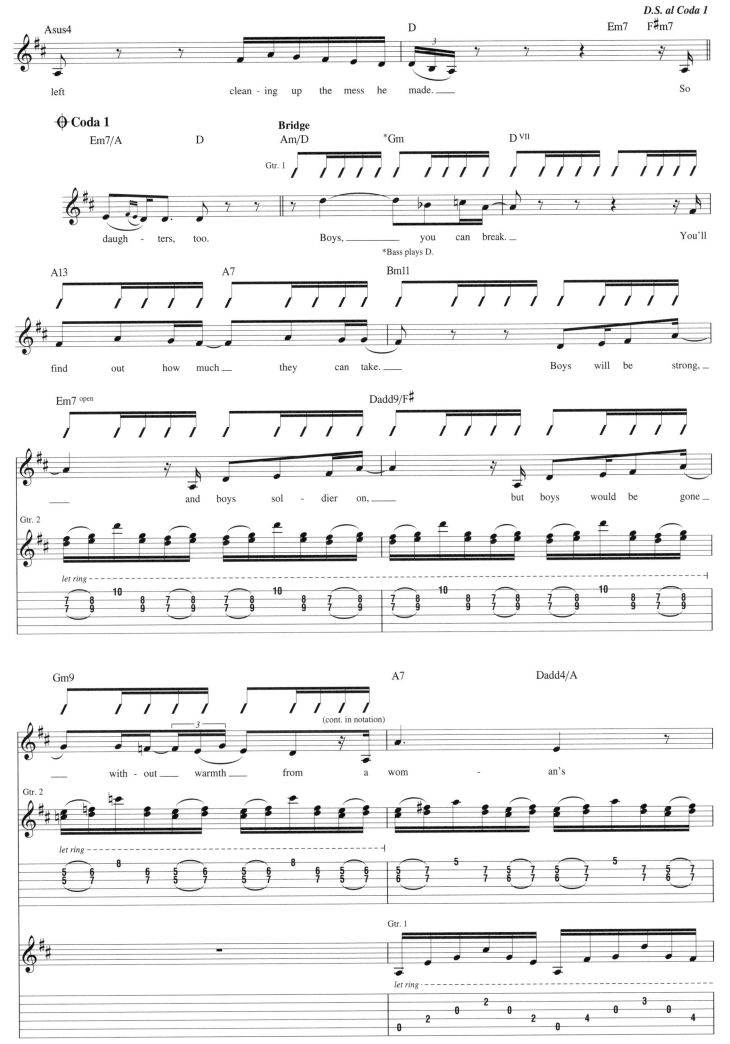

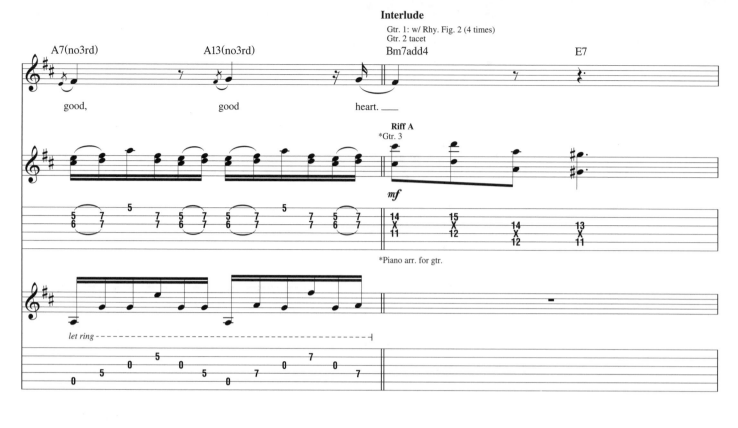

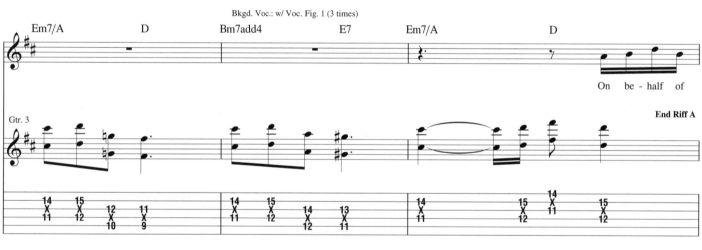

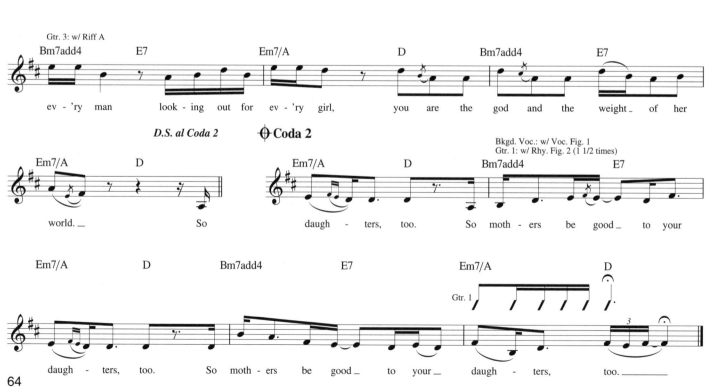

ONLY HEART

Words and Music by
John Mayer

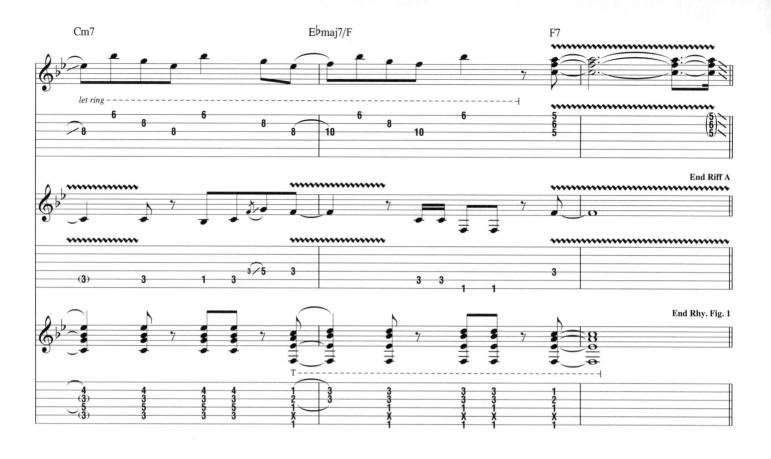

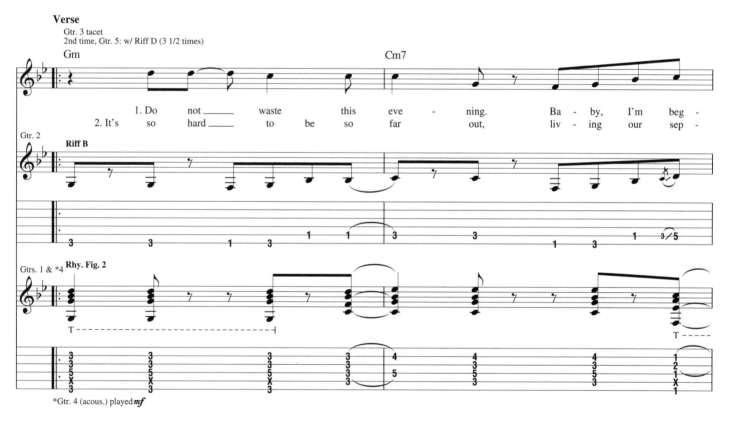

*Gtr. 4 (acous.) played **mf***

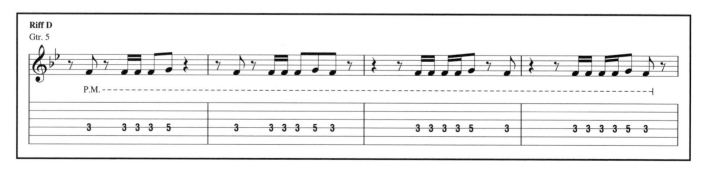

Gtrs. 1 & 4: w/ Rhy. Fig. 2 (2 times)
Gtr. 2: w/ Riff B (2 1/2 times)

You big ___ i - mag - i - na - tion's play - ing its tricks ___
Your phone ___ was real - ly bro - ken. I tried your num -

___ on you
- ber twice.

if you think ___ my up and
And if you ___ need con - fir -

leav - ing's some - thing I'm gon - na do.
ma - tion, ba - by, I un - der - stand.

Feel my chest ___ when I look at you. Ba - by, you, ___
It's al - right ___ if you want me to tell you. You, ___

Gtrs. 1 & 4

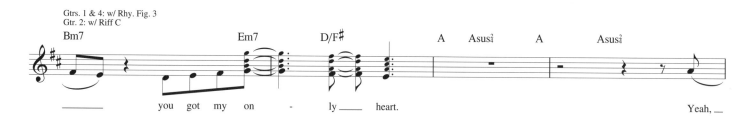

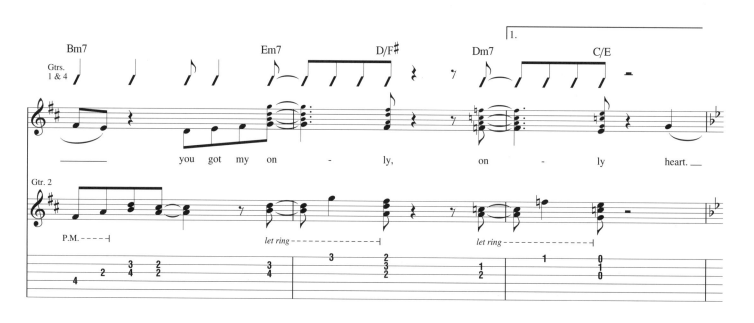

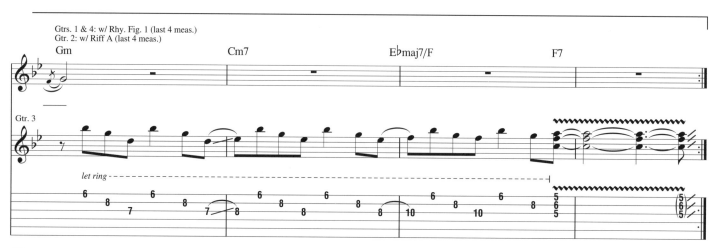

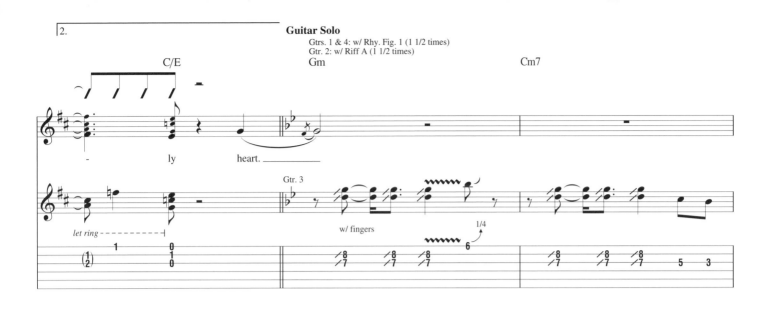

Guitar Solo
Gtrs. 1 & 4: w/ Rhy. Fig. 1 (1 1/2 times)
Gtr. 2: w/ Riff A (1 1/2 times)

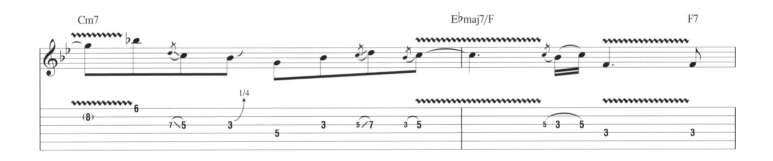

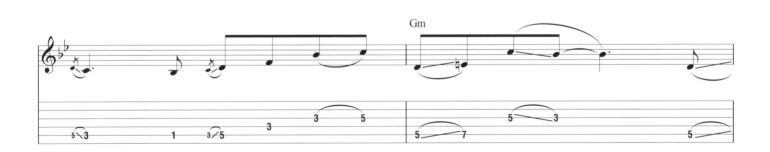

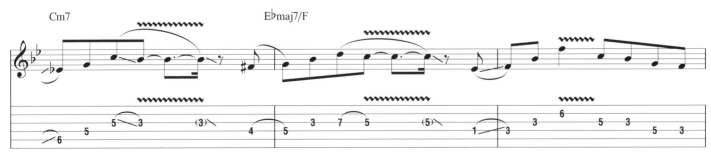

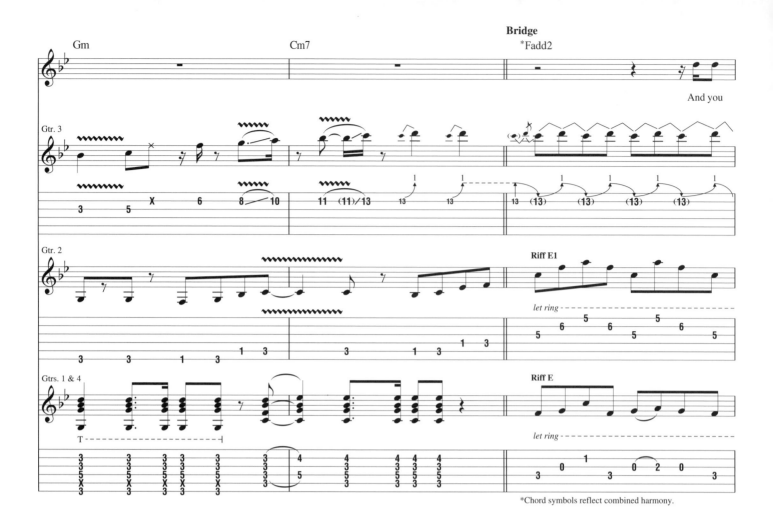

*Chord symbols reflect combined harmony.

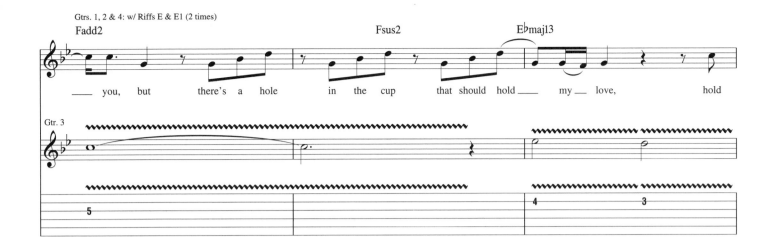

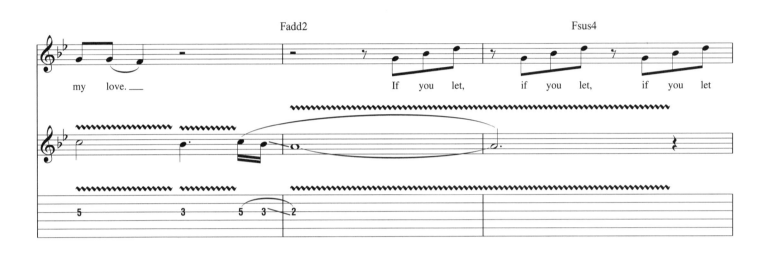

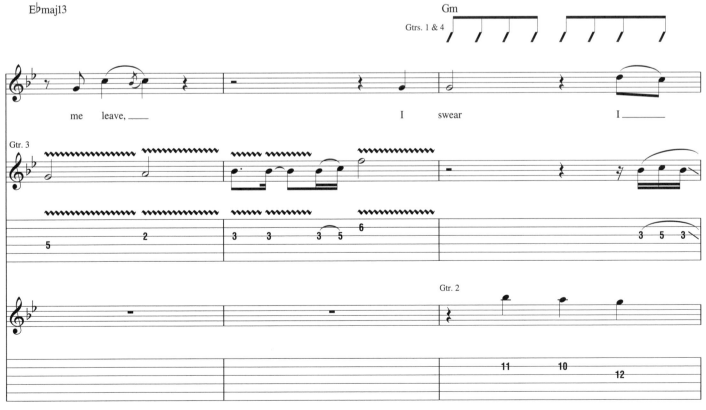

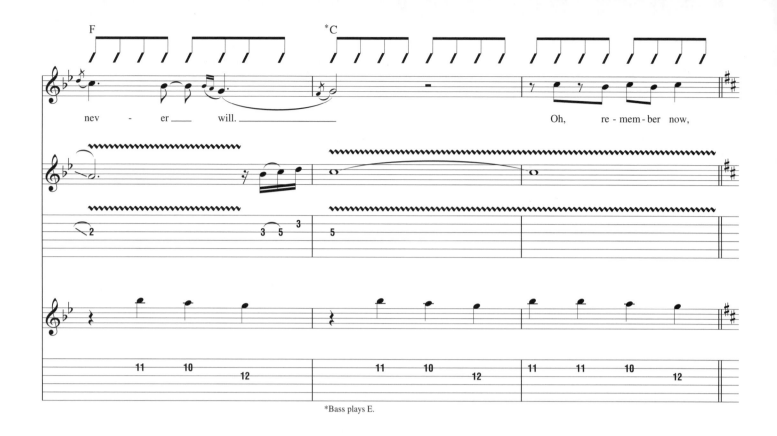

*Bass plays E.

Chorus

Gtrs. 1 & 4: w/ Rhy. Fig. 3 (2 times)
Gtr. 2: w/ Riff C (2 times)
Gtr. 3 tacet

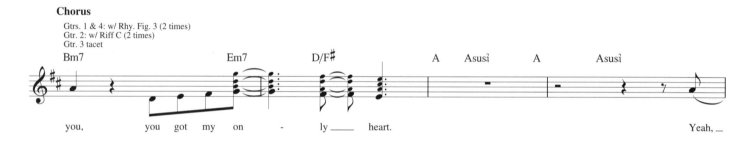

you, you got my on - ly ___ heart. Yeah, ___

you got my on - ly ___ heart. Yeah, ___

Gtr. 2: w/ Riff A (1st 4 meas.)

Repeat and fade

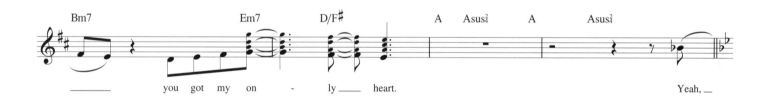

you got my on - ly ___ heart. Yeah, ___

Gtrs. 1 & 3

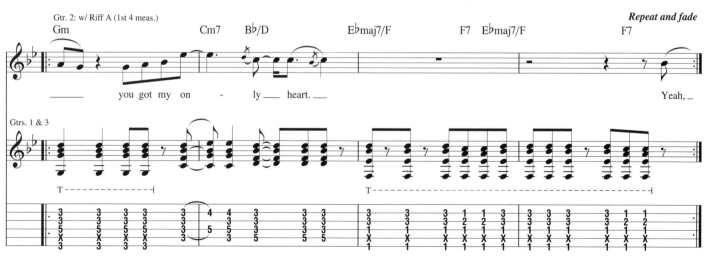

WHEEL

Words and Music by
John Mayer

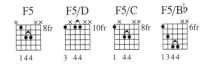

Intro
Slowly, in 2 ♩ = 64

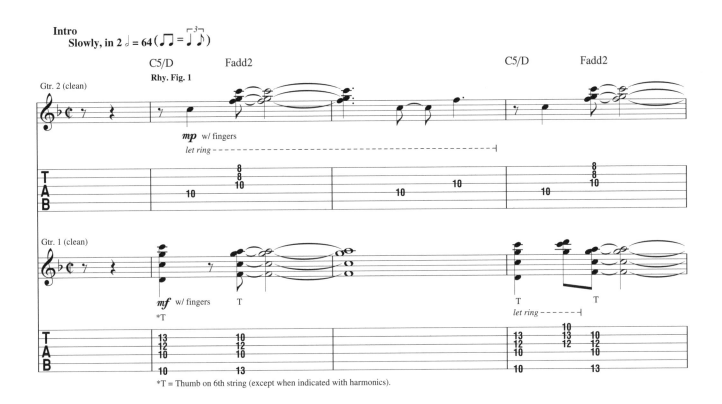

*T = Thumb on 6th string (except when indicated with harmonics).

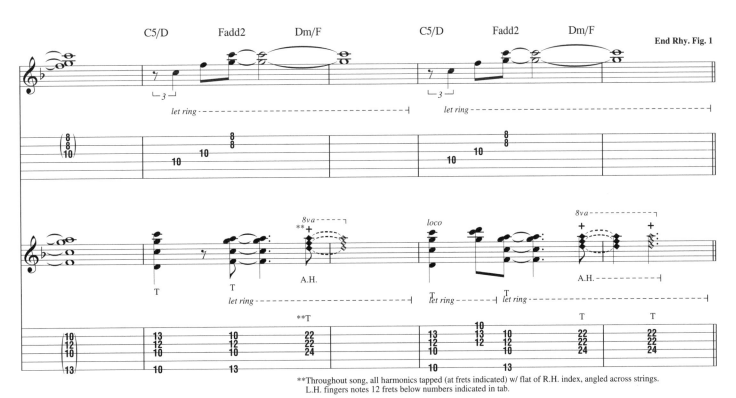

**Throughout song, all harmonics tapped (at frets indicated) w/ flat of R.H. index, angled across strings.
L.H. fingers notes 12 frets below numbers indicated in tab.

Verse

Gtr. 2: w/ Rhy. Fig. 1

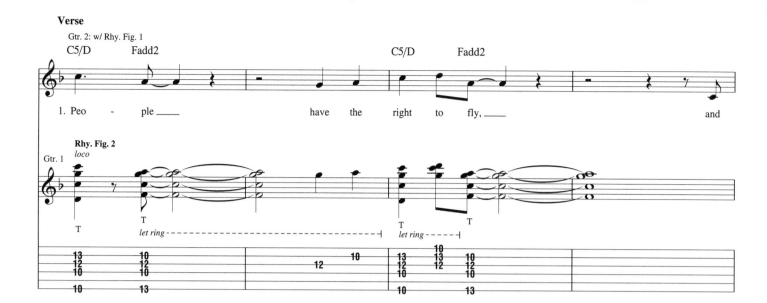

1. Peo - ple _____ have the right to fly, _____ and

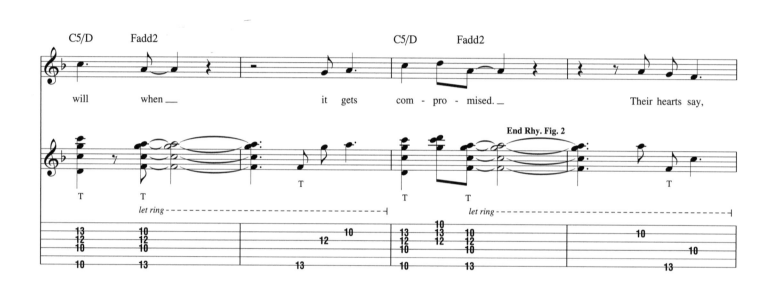

will when _____ it gets com - pro - mised. __ Their hearts say,

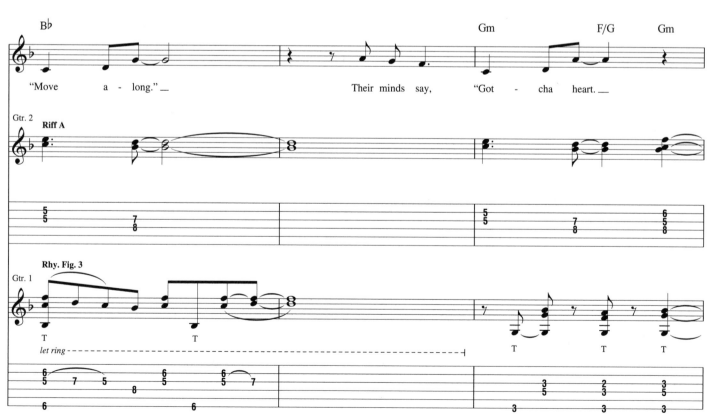

"Move a - long." __ Their minds say, "Got - cha heart. __

74

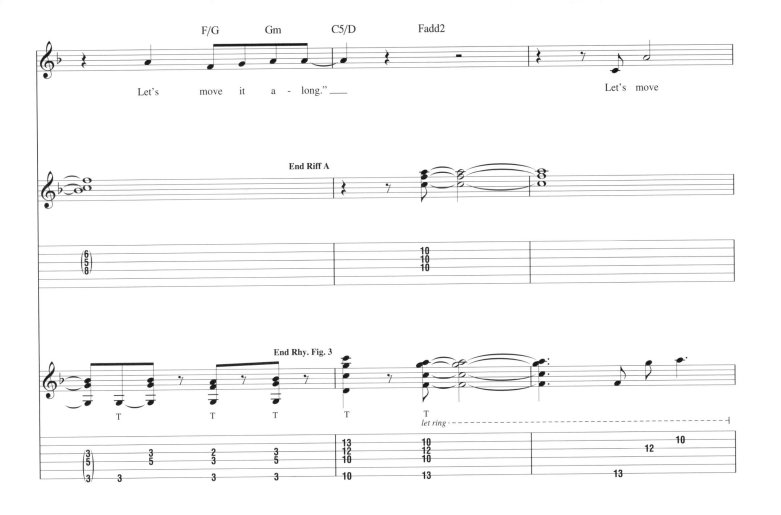

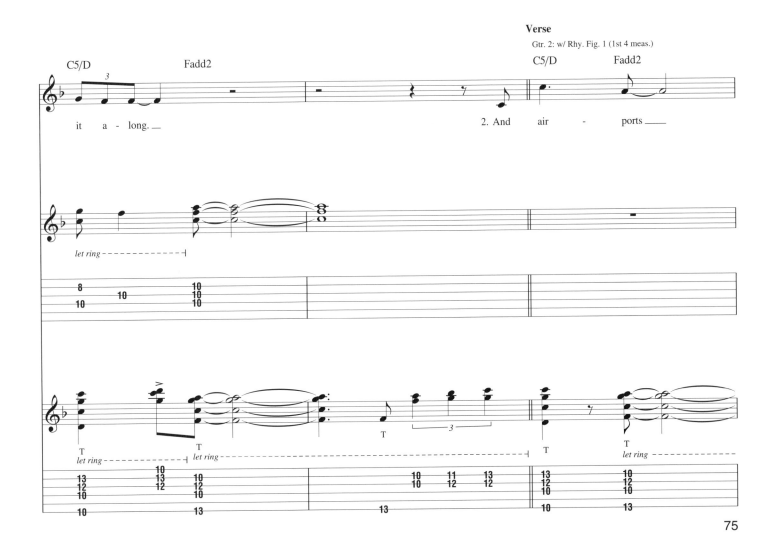

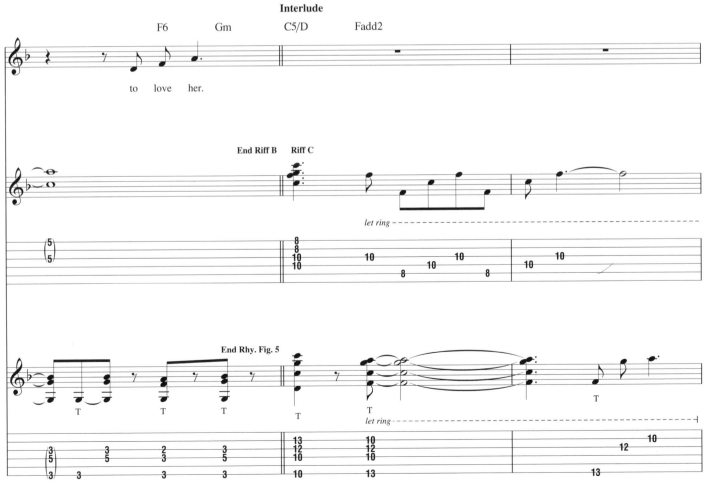

*Played as even eight notes.

Verse

Gtr. 1: w/ Rhy. Fig. 2
Gtr. 2: w/ Riff C (last 2 meas.) (4 times)

3. You can't ___ build a house of leaves ___ and

live like ___ it's an ev - er - green. ___

Gtr. 2: w/ Riff A

It's just a sea - son thing. ___ It's just ___ this thing ___

78

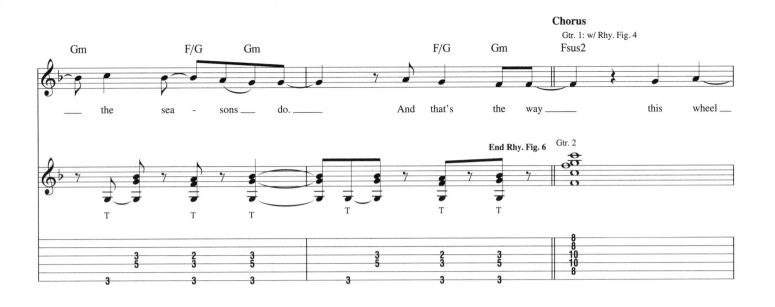

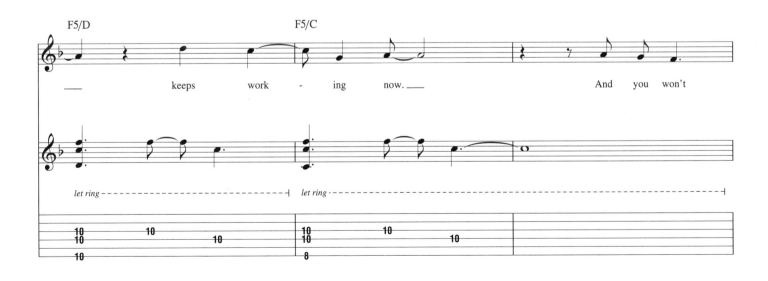

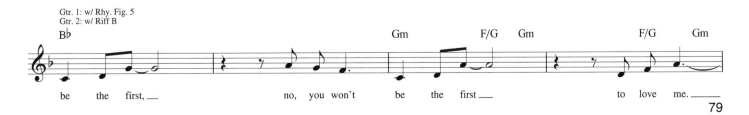

79

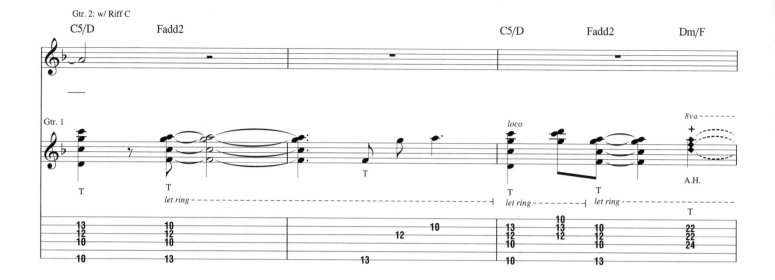

Guitar Solo

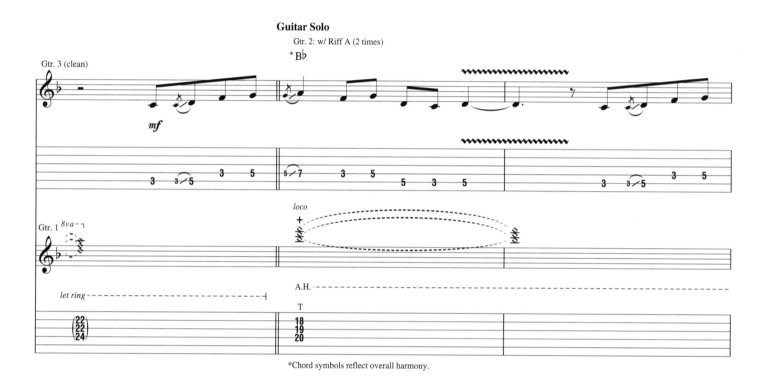

*Chord symbols reflect overall harmony.

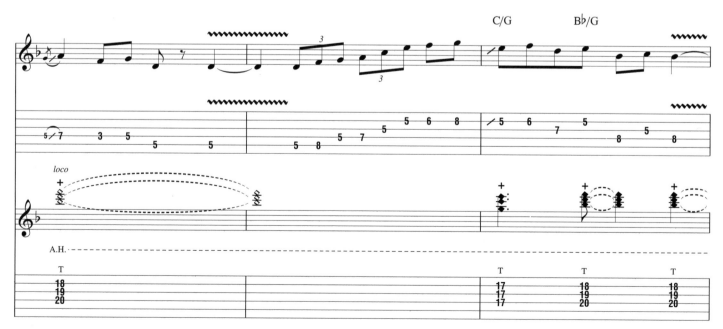

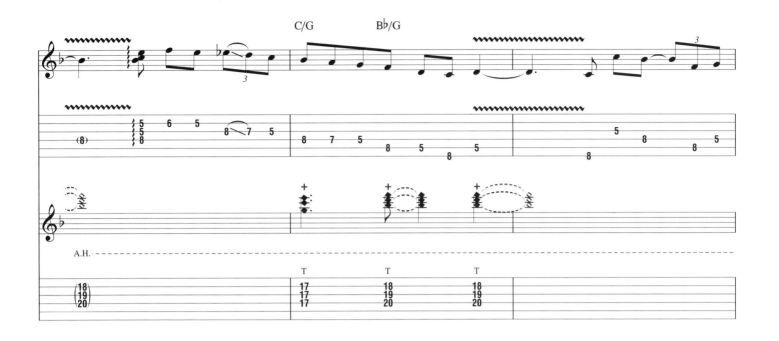

Gtr. 2: w/ Riff C (last 2 meas.) (2 times)

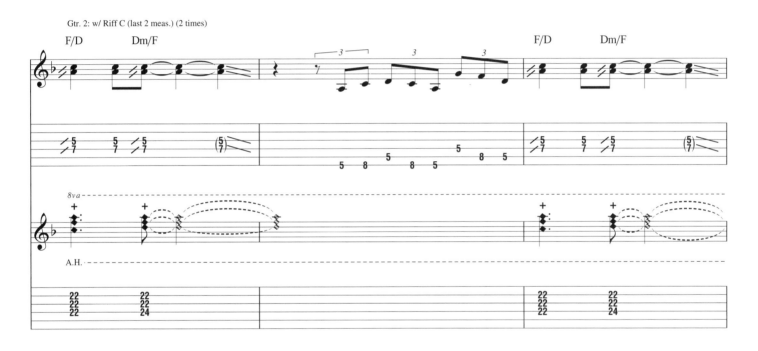

Gtr. 2: w/ Riff A

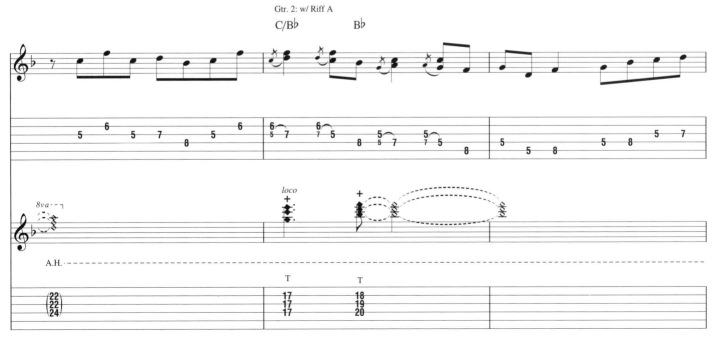

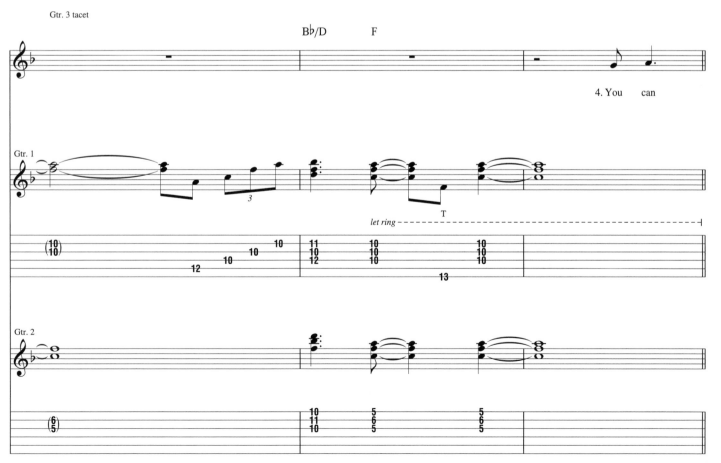

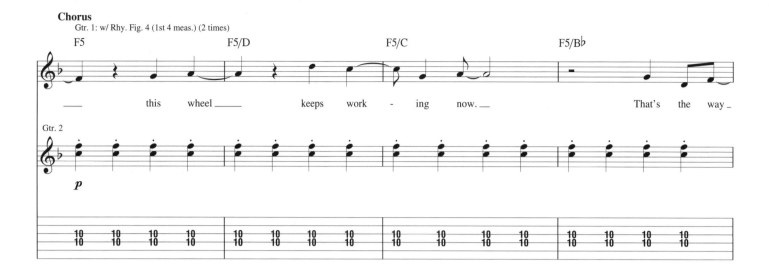

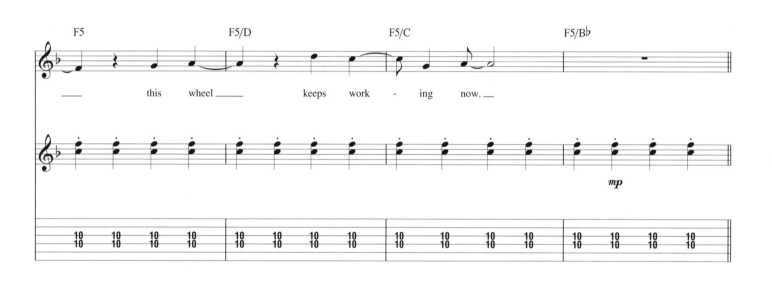

Outro

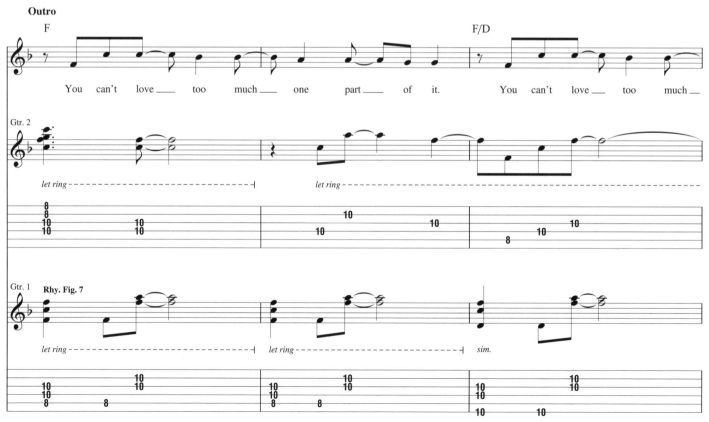

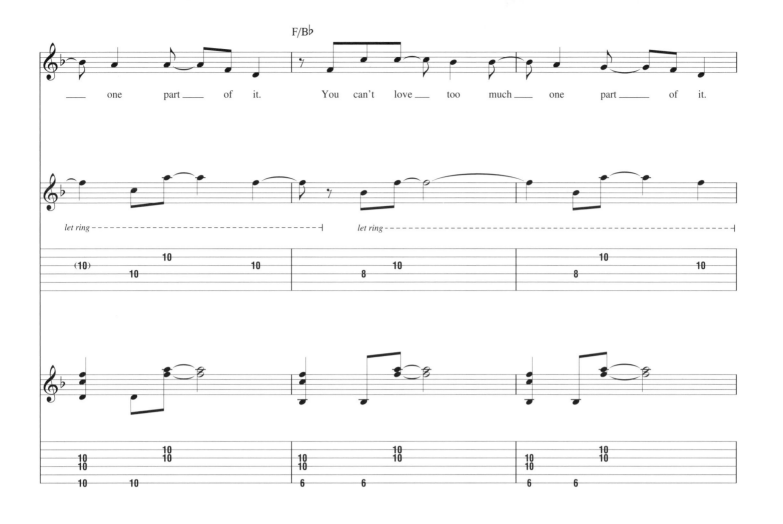

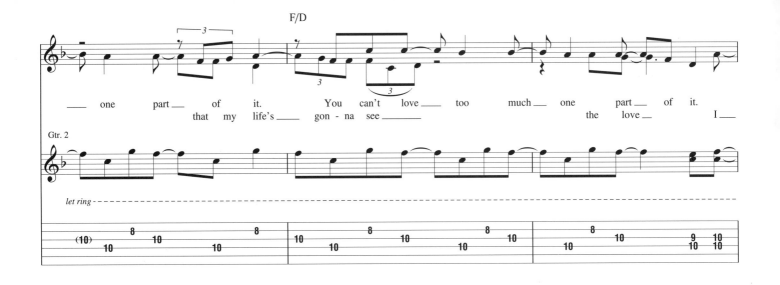

one part of it. You can't love too much one part of it.
that my life's gonna see the love I

You can't love too much one part of it. You can't love too much
give returned to me.

one part of it. You can't love too much one part of it.
I believe that my life's

Guitar Notation Legend

Guitar Music can be notated three different ways: on a *musical staff*, in *tablature*, and in *rhythm slashes*.

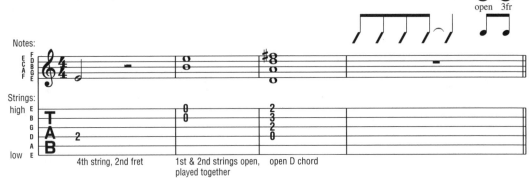

RHYTHM SLASHES are written above the staff. Strum chords in the rhythm indicated. Use the chord diagrams found at the top of the first page of the transcription for the appropriate chord voicings. Round noteheads indicate single notes.

THE MUSICAL STAFF shows pitches and rhythms and is divided by bar lines into measures. Pitches are named after the first seven letters of the alphabet.

TABLATURE graphically represents the guitar fingerboard. Each horizontal line represents a string, and each number represents a fret.

4th string, 2nd fret   1st & 2nd strings open, played together   open D chord

---

HALF-STEP BEND: Strike the note and bend up 1/2 step.

WHOLE-STEP BEND: Strike the note and bend up one step.

GRACE NOTE BEND: Strike the note and immediately bend up as indicated.

SLIGHT (MICROTONE) BEND: Strike the note and bend up 1/4 step.

BEND AND RELEASE: Strike the note and bend up as indicated, then release back to the original note. Only the first note is struck.

PRE-BEND: Bend the note as indicated, then strike it.

VIBRATO: The string is vibrated by rapidly bending and releasing the note with the fretting hand.

WIDE VIBRATO: The pitch is varied to a greater degree by vibrating with the fretting hand.

HAMMER-ON: Strike the first (lower) note with one finger, then sound the higher note (on the same string) with another finger by fretting it without picking.

PULL-OFF: Place both fingers on the notes to be sounded. Strike the first note and without picking, pull the finger off to sound the second (lower) note.

LEGATO SLIDE: Strike the first note and then slide the same fret-hand finger up or down to the second note. The second note is not struck.

SHIFT SLIDE: Same as legato slide, except the second note is struck.

TRILL: Very rapidly alternate between the notes indicated by continuously hammering on and pulling off.

TAPPING: Hammer ("tap") the fret indicated with the pick-hand index or middle finger and pull off to the note fretted by the fret hand.

NATURAL HARMONIC: Strike the note while the fret-hand lightly touches the string directly over the fret indicated.

PINCH HARMONIC: The note is fretted normally and a harmonic is produced by adding the edge of the thumb or the tip of the index finger of the pick hand to the normal pick attack.

PICK SCRAPE: The edge of the pick is rubbed down (or up) the string, producing a scratchy sound.

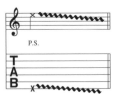

MUFFLED STRINGS: A percussive sound is produced by laying the fret hand across the string(s) without depressing, and striking them with the pick hand.

PALM MUTING: The note is partially muted by the pick hand lightly touching the string(s) just before the bridge.

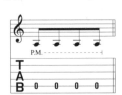

RAKE: Drag the pick across the strings indicated with a single motion.

TREMOLO PICKING: The note is picked as rapidly and continuously as possible.

VIBRATO BAR DIVE AND RETURN: The pitch of the note or chord is dropped a specified number of steps (in rhythm) then returned to the original pitch.

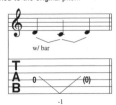

VIBRATO BAR SCOOP: Depress the bar just before striking the note, then quickly release the bar.

VIBRATO BAR DIP: Strike the note and then immediately drop a specified number of steps, then release back to the original pitch.